# Testimony

## STAR STEVENS

Dorrance Publishing Co
585 Alpha Drive
Suite 103
Pittsburgh, PA 15238
Visit our website at www.dorrancebookstore.com

ISBN: 979-8-88812-101-6
eISBN: 979-8-88812-601-1

This book is dedicated to all of those who suffer in silence. Hoping that one day they'll find peace and happiness in their lives.

This story is about how one girl suffered greatly, and went from broken to healed. Within this book, there will be talks about physical, mental, spiritual, and emotional abuse. This book will hold my old traumas and will not hold back any detail or alleviate any story. They will come directly from source. I pray that those who read this book do not take pity on me but finds strength in my strength to carry on another day.

By creating this book, I have chosen to share all the dirty secrets of my past, in hopes that it is the light for someone else. This book is not intended to make anyone angry, nor cause anyone harm, and in no way am I asking anyone to hate anyone this book is based on. You will see while reading this book that I am not that type of person. With that said, I will be changing the names of all the characters except my own.

This book is based on true events. Aside from the character's names, this book is 100% non-fictional. I know that some of the things I mention might seem fictional, however I guarantee you I experienced all these events down to the details. So please continue reading with an open mind, and a heart that is free from judgement.

# CHAPTER 1

# The Beginning

**In order to start this book off right,** I must start from my oldest memory.

Tosha was a few months pregnant carrying what she hadn't known would be her last two children, Mina and me. I would become her seventh child birthed into this world. While awaiting my arrival into this new world, I remember being in a dark place. Well, not that dark. I could see light trying to make its way through Tasha's skin, like what you'd see closing your eyes and looking at your eyelids. I remember seeing what I would later understand them to be as two spirits in my mother's womb. They both entered my body, then I entered. I do not remember coming out of the womb nor the steps after.

Tosha was on heavy drugs after giving birth, so she gave my sister and me to two different homes. I went to my godmother and my twin to another home. Later, my godmother would find my twin and raise us both. Over the years, I gained the reputation of being my papa's favorite grandchild and became very close to him.

*This next part is very serious, and therefore I do not support or take part in gaslighting.*

I remember times when my nana and I would get in fights about my papa, and she would say she was done with him, and she found a new man. She would walk us to a room and present my papa again as if he had changed. He would buy us things and take care of us well, which I now understand would be gifts so that we would keep our mouths shut about what was really happening to us. We were so young that now those memories are just fragments and the only reason they still exist is because I cling to them.

Besides the fact that I was younger than six while in their care, my nana and papa were my favorite people. I loved cooking with them, folding clothes, cleaning, and playing in the yard. I always loved to help around the house whenever I could and to sit and watch old cowboy movies with my nana. One day when I was six, our birth mother Tosha came, and she was playing Irreplaceable by Beyonce. We sang and danced, happy to see her. I remember the car being big and the music booming. Mina and I hopped in the car and went with Tosha.

Tosha bought us push pops and we sat in the back of the car riding for miles to a new city. I always fall asleep on car rides. When I woke up, we were at Tosha's town house in a city called Raleigh.

I remember the first thing I did was tell Tosha about the sexual abuse that happened while we lived with our godparents. I remember laying in the bed while Papa did things that I cannot now really remember, but when I was six, I knew what happened. She made it clear that she would investigate, and we would never get harmed in her care. I also remember when we got babysat, the babysitter would lock us in the closet and make us suck on one of our cousin's penis or she wouldn't let us out. I never told Tosha about this because it wasn't something I saw as wrong during that time. I understand now why I grew up interested in sex.

Everything was perfect. We went to Millbrook Elementary, and we had friends in our neighborhood. Tosha was single for a while, and she worked three jobs. When she was off, she would take us on trips to amusement parks and out to eat. I loved watching her cook and would sometimes pretend she was on a cooking channel. My favorite meal for her to prepare was spaghetti, Texas toast, and salad. The smell of the buttery toast and tomato sauce filled the house. That's when I knew it would be a great day. I would sit at the dinner table, kicking my feet and wiggling in my chair as I ate. Tosha called it my happy dance and she loved to watch me dance as I ate, because that is how she knew the meal was good.

My childhood with Tosha in the beginning wasn't that bad. Dominic and I loved playing together. We played outside in the woods behind our house like we were fighting unseen enemies and monsters. We would jump across a river and claim territories. His friends would join us and we'd sword fight with sticks. Sometimes we would stay inside and play video games. He'd teach me how to play Madden, but my favorite game to play was Naruto. This was before I knew anything about the anime, which is now one of my favorite animes. I remember placing the game into his PlayStation One and watching the game load up. His favorite thing to do was use a jutsu to put me to sleep while he beat me up. When I did beat him, he'd smile and say, "I let you win." Dominic was one of my favorite people.

Whenever Tosha's birthday would roll around, I loved making her handwritten letters and poems to demonstrate the love that I had for her. When holiday seasons came, we'd spend more time as a family, and I loved that the most. Sitting with my family, joking around, playing board games, and letting the nights pass us by. After a few years passed, we became a family that didn't celebrate holidays or birthdays. I'm guessing money got tight and we couldn't afford to pay for gifts and the bills, so Tosha decided to pay the bills.

Meeting and living with Tosha in those first few years weren't bad. I could tell she was trying hard to be a good mother. Though she had no examples. She was giving us the life she thought a good mother would give to her children. However, that all came falling apart when she met my birth father again.

# CHAPTER 2

# Broken Home

**Tosha had met back up with Anthony,** the man who got her on the drugs in the first place. You could say Tosha was Anthony's Harley Quinn. She would do anything for him, even crack-cocaine. He was someone she loved, and she wanted to give him another chance to prove he loved her. They got married and he moved in. Those initial moments were my favorite. Anthony worked at a hotdog shack, and we would go visit him. He would always give us free food and ice cream. My favorite at the time was rocky road. We'd sit at the picnic tables, the sun beaming down on us as our ice cream melted, and we talked about how our days went. I remember the smile he had on his face while we approached the stand. I loved him and he had become another favorite person in my life.

After a while, the drug abuse problem surfaced, and Tosha refused, stating that she wanted to raise her children and did not need to be back on those drugs. In fact, we were the reason she found the strength to quit. He got mad and started abusing her. I was coming up the stairs after hearing my mother scream. I watched as he dragged her into their room, and she yelled, "Call the cops." I became frozen in fear as I watched him drag her through the door and to the edge of the bed. He looked up at me and dropped her, then chased me into my room and slammed the door. All I could do was cry as I heard my mother get beat in the other room. I cried at the fact that I was powerless, and I couldn't save my own mother.

We continued to live as if nothing ever happened. We went out as a family to the park, and we had memorable times together. One night, Anthony came into the room with an antenna on his head, pretending to be an alien. He chased us around the room until we got into our beds. We talked for a while, then they kissed us good-night and left. Mina and I would stay up and play games like guess that song as the other hummed the melody, or we would draw pic-ture on each other's back while the other tried to guess the picture.

I do not remember when this happened, but one day as Anthony was headed out, he mentioned that he didn't love us, he only loved Tosha. After that, we saw him in a different light.

One day, Anthony forgot to come home, and my mother thought he was out cheating, so she threw all his stuff out and had the locks changed. I'm guessing this was the straw that broke the camel's back, because when he returned, my mother called the cops. I remember the cops asking us if our father had returned home that night, and we said, "No." Truthfully, I didn't remember anything; I just said what Tosha had prepped us to say if they asked. After talking with the cops, they informed Anthony that he couldn't return and that he had to find another place to live. They later got a divorce and Tosha began dating again.

Mina and I were upstairs in our room when she called us down to meet her new boyfriend, David. He was Hispanic and a gentle-man. Something I'll never forget was looking him in the eye as he handed me twenty dollars. He started shaking and became nervous as he approached me. Tosha said I had an intimidating stare and that I shouldn't make eye contact with people. Then he chatted with her and left. She asked us how we liked him; she had a big smile on her face and seemed to be happy to date him. However, after that day, I never saw him again. She didn't mention a breakup; it was just on to the next.

Darius was her next boyfriend, and he had a daughter who was two years old at the time. Her name was Mikayla. They moved in; getting used to not being the youngest was weird to me. I had to take care of someone and protect her. One day, I was sitting at the top of the stairs and Mikayla was climbing them to come give me a hug. When she reached the top, we hugged, and she started to lean back. Even at nine, I knew that was a bad idea, but I couldn't just let her go and protect myself. I had to keep her from falling as well. I yelled for my twin Mina, but she was too slow. Mikayla and I began falling down the stairs. I wrapped my body around her and held on tight. When we reached the bottom, Tosha and Darius were already there and Tosha looked furious. I got beat for dropping Mikayla, when the truth was, I didn't; in fact, I protected her even while we were falling. After that, Darius became a no-call, no-show.

I learned that love was tricky and that anything could break it if the love weren't strong enough. I knew that I wouldn't have kids and that I would become successful. I loved writing and singing, and I knew that for me, love wasn't my main goal in life; success was.

I had two other sisters named Zina and Sasha. Sasha came to live with us for a while. She basically raised us part-time. If we were to get in trouble or do something bad, she'd have us do wall squats. I remember one time she had me do a wall squat while she walked to the store. I tried to stay up the whole time, but I ended up sitting down. When she got back, I got back up and she looked at me, surprised. She had forgotten that she told me to do them. Sasha and I would get in petty arguments about little things. That's what sisters do.

Our oldest brother Rick came around and he gave me my first cigarette. We sat under the balcony of our townhouse smoking. Later, we went inside and hung out with him. He showed sexual interest in Mina and me. He even tried to rape Mina in the butt, thinking she would let him. She stopped him and told him to leave. We didn't mention this to Tosha until weeks after, but there was no point. He was still welcomed to come and go as he pleased.

I understood that sexual abuse was another thing my family suffered with, as Tosha was abused by her own father as well.

# CHAPTER 3

# The Abuse

**It wasn't long after Tosha's streak of** singleness that the abuse started. First, it was just words. I broke one of her lamps because I was swinging around and singing on it. She came downstairs to beat me for breaking the lamp and told me that my brain was as big as a thumb tack hole in the wall. She didn't refrain from calling me a bitch whenever she could. This was when I learned that the past has a way of masking itself as personality traits or characteristics. She used the fact that we needed her against us and made it clear we wouldn't survive without her. I didn't think it could get worse, but I was sadly mistaken.

After a couple years passed, we moved back to Salisbury and began attending Knox Middle in a new neighborhood, trying to make friends.

One day, my brother and I were outside playing when a lady claimed that Dominic had hit her child. I ran upstairs to our apartment and told Tosha, "They're trying to say that Dominic hit Paris." She looked at me with rage in her eyes and drug me by my hair into the house, punching me in the face. She continued dragging and punching me until we ended up in the kitchen. My cousin Max screamed, "Hit her with an open hand! Hit her with an open hand!" That day, I learned that abuse was common in my family. After she let me go, I ran into my room, crying and rocking myself.

That day, the daydreams began. I would dream that Robin from *Teen Titans* would come save me and that I wouldn't have to suffer anymore. I dreamed that I would have superpowers and that everyone who hurt me would regret it. I found comfort in those dreams, and I would have them often.

We moved from that neighborhood to live with my grandma Alicia. That's when I learned that my grandma abused my mother and that she still hadn't forgiven her for it. We slept on a futon and my mother slept on the floor. I hated living there, because before then, I never knew what a roach was. Tosha wouldn't just hit me; she would punch Dominic if he talked back and once tried to snap Mina's neck. The abuse got heavy after we moved in with Alicia. Somehow, Alicia convinced Tosha that Dominic had to go to a group home because he couldn't be controlled. I lost one of my favorite people that day.

After a while, Mina and I started getting in trouble at school. We called the cafeteria worker gay on the camera that was on the bus and claimed that anyone who ate his hair would turn gay. When Tosha found out, she beat us with a charging cord along with switches. Mina and I cried together for the first time. We were suspended for three days and had to clean and take care of the house.

We moved to an apartment that was close to our godparents and we visited them often. This is when the topic of rape resurfaced, and my nana claimed it never happened. Tosha told us it never happened and that we made it up. We were told to apologize to our papa, and from then on, I couldn't trust my own thoughts on the matter.

*Gaslighting might fix the situation then, but for the victim, it leaves them confused and lost, forced to think that they cannot trust themselves anymore, even if they know for a fact that event or situation took place.*

We basically stayed at our godparent's house and would go home to sleep and for school. One day, I found a pregnancy test in the bathroom at my god mom's house, and I took it home. Before I took a bath, I took it and waited for the results. I remember wrapping it in tissue and sitting it beside the tub. I knew I never had sex; in fact I hadn't even started my period, but I was a curious child with the need to know. I forgot that I had taken it and left it beside the tub. The next day I went to school, came home, and went outside to play. Tosha found the pregnancy test and was waiting for me to come back in. When I did, she began punching me in the face and dragging me to the ground. She stomped on my stomach and threw a fan at me, screaming that I better not be pregnant.

I cried, "I'm not!" as she finished her last blow and walked away. I went to my dog Codi which my godmother had given me and cried while holding him. He was my best friend, and he always made me happy. That night, I daydreamed about being super powerful and watching those who hurt me beg for forgiveness. I prayed for happier days and cried myself to sleep.

A year went by, and now we were in a new house and attending North Rowan Middle.

*I should mention that these memories are blurry as I'm telling them in the order I remember. They could've happened in a different timeline; however, they did occur.*

I was always able to hear and see spirits that roam the earth. That is how I was born. Tosha claimed that we could talk to angels. She would constantly tell us to talk to angels and ask them questions for her. Mina and I did our best to give her answers that she wanted to hear. One day I told her something that she didn't like, and she said I talked to demons and that I should pray that gift away. I did as I was told but regretted it. Tosha was a heavy Christian and she hated anything or anyone who didn't obey God's word.

Tosha met a man she knew in the past named Ever. She then went on to marry him and he moved in. I was no longer the youngest again. This time I had two younger brothers and that was fine with me. Dominic came back and we had a happy time together. We went to the beach for the first time and to Ripley's Believe it or Not. Dominic said he didn't want to go so he didn't get to go. When he found out we went to the beach, he was hurt.

Time went by and weed was introduced to us. I remember climbing on Tosha's bed and knocking something down. Later that day, she asked us what happened to her weed. We didn't know any-thing about it. She said that Dominic had stolen and smoked it, and she beat him with a broomstick. Later, I mentioned knocking it off her bed while grabbing something, and she beat me because she was upset that she had beaten Dominic and wrapped a wire around my neck.

*Even now I don't know if the wire part took place because it is a blurry memory, but I do remember that day.*

I cried and apologized to her.

I remember seeing a spirit or demon in a window of our house. Mina claimed to see one as well. However, hers looked nothing like what I had seen. It was just a black entity with red eyes. Mina saw something like a clown with swirls for eyes dancing around the room. Tosha took this very seriously and told us to tell her if we ever saw them again.

One night, Mina and I were laying in the room with my little brother and my little cousin Tuda. Our brother Ever Jr. wanted to have sex with Mina, but she told him if he wanted her, he'd have to have sex with Tuda. I sat and watched as an instigator as Ever Jr. had sex with Tuda and after that he went to clean himself. The next morning, Tuda was rushed to the hospital because his butthole was bleeding. We knew what had happened and we convinced Ever Jr. to say that Dominic told him to do it. Dominic was sent to a group home again. After, we found out he wanted to kill himself.

Once Dominic was gone, we were distant from our younger brothers and stayed more to ourselves. I remember Ever leaving with his finger on his mouth and I thought he was telling me to be quiet. I ran in the house and told Tosha what I had seen. She got angry and pushed the refrigerator. I found out that she thought he was cheating on her the whole time. She got drunk and broke the fish tank which was home to many fish. He came home and they cleared the air.

I got into a fight and for the first time I would stand up for my-self. I ended up fighting a girl on the bus for talking about me. One girl stated that she would fight me. She felt bad that I fought her, because I was bigger than her. I looked at her in fear but knowing that if she did, I would try to kill her. I got suspended and received an assault charge. I had to do community service. I swore I would never fight again.

Some time had passed and Ever inherited a house and some land, and because he was married, Tosha became partial owner as well. We would go and spend days up there as he fixed the house. One day, while we were sitting at home Tosha went to the new house in Cleveland, NC. There she would catch Ever cheating on her with another woman. She started to dent his car with a hammer. Instead, she stopped herself and filed for a divorce. We got the land and the house and Ever and his two sons moved back with his ex.

We forgot about the house in Cleveland and Tosha bought a house in East Spencer, NC. We now attended North Rowan High School.

# CHAPTER 4

# Deep Wounds

**A new house that no one could put us out of.** Tosha had bought a house, so we never had to move again. I walked out on to the porch as I watched my older brother throw up gang signs to a passing car and I yelled, "Stop throwing those gang signs up at this house!" Tosha grabbed my hair and drug me into the house, punching and kicking me. I was confused on what I had done now as she punched me in the face, I cried. Later, she said she thought I had screamed, "We gangbang at this house." Or something of the sort. She always apologized after abusing me and I would always forgive her.

After a while, I began neglecting Codi and he passed away. This broke my heart into pieces. Rick came and helped me bury him. I made a little cross out of two wooden boards and put it on his grave.

Tosha was adamant on living like Jesus. That meant no running water and no regular lights. We had to use rainwater that we caught to bathe and if the barrels were empty, we had to use water bottles. We only cooked on a kerosene heater, and it had to be cold. She didn't want to waste money on kerosene. We had solar power so if it were cloudy or if it rained, it meant no lights. We could flush the toilet by dumping a bucket of water in it. If it were clogged, poop and urine would pile up in the toilet. Keep in mind, there were three girls and one man living in this house. Which meant if someone were on their period, and it got clogged, you would smell it. When I had to poo, I would just go outside with some tissue and squat.

I would sleep with Tosha and rub her feet while she fell asleep, or I would tell her stories until she fell asleep. When she got sick, I would take care of her and if I didn't, she'd claim we didn't love her. I was the only one who stepped up to care for her. I would sleep in the living room with her. She'd sleep on the couch or on the recliner and I'd sleep on the floor. I could hear mice running around on the floor. I would just ball up and tuck the cover under me so they couldn't get in. I was responsible for removing the mice after they got caught. If a squirrel died in the water barrels that we used to catch rainwater, I would have to remove them as well. My favorite parts during this time were watching movies on the TV when we could.

Many times, I would plot to kill her while she was sleep. I never brought myself to do it. When I wanted to spend time alone, she would call me selfish. When my brother moved out, I got my own room. I had to clean his room after he left, so she could move into it. I moved to the room that was all the way in the back. I remember she would call me, and I did not hear a thing. Like I was standing in matter, and nothing could pierce it. One time I had sleep paralysis and a dark figure with horns stood in the doorway. I always knew there was another side so that did not scare me. It wouldn't be the last time I would see the entity.

Whenever we were in the car, and I'd say something she didn't like she'd punch me in the face. Or if we did something bad and I sat up front, she'd punch me in the face. I'm not just talking one time either she'd do it multiple times. Then say, "Put your hand down, making people think I'm hurting you." Whenever I would cry, she would send me away saying that she couldn't handle emotions.

My favorite time of the year was soccer season. I had played in eighth grade and had intentions on playing my freshmen year. I tried out and made the team. Coach Wing Wing became one of my favorite people. I loved soccer; I could take out my aggression on the field. Even though we never won a game my teammates and I never gave up. The girls took care of me, and always gave me rides if they could. If not, I would walk home. I used to beg Tosha to come to my games, but she didn't care, saying that we never won a game. She'd only go to Dominic's football games.

A year went by, and Mina joined the band. Tosha loved music, so she participated heavily with the band buying snacks and helping after school. I became the band assistant and helped. One day, my sister passed out at the game and was rushed to the hospital. Tosha found out that Mina was anemic. Mina's best friend at the time told Tosha that I had eaten her food and that was why she was malnourished that day. The truth was, Mina wasn't going to eat and even threatened to throw the food away and I was still hungry. Tosha was mad at me and told me I couldn't play soccer or be the assistant anymore. She said we never won a game anyways, so it didn't matter. I begged to be back on the team and eventually she let me.

Sasha moved back in with us, and we would get into fights about things I hadn't done. She screamed at me, saying that the way I looked at her it seemed like I wanted to swing on her. I held my anger in, trying not to hit anyone that I loved.

I began watching anime and hanging around the band kids. I learned how to play chess and I started to enjoy my life a little more. I would accidentally break things and get beat for it. I hated going home, not knowing if I'd get punched for breathing too hard or looking her in the eyes. Would I get kicked for saying the wrong things or chewing too loudly? That is what my life became, living in constant fear of the one person who promised to protect us.

*The following is one of my deepest traumas and it took me a long time to dig this trauma out. It is completely true and none of the details are exaggerated.*

One day, Tosha's toothbrush went missing and she blamed Mina and me for misplacing it. She began punching us and screaming like a maniac. She would punch on me asking, "Where is my toothbrush!" repeatedly. I screamed I didn't know, which was the truth, because I didn't. She then grabbed a screwdriver and began stabbing me with it all over my body. I screamed begging her to stop. I remember saying, "I don't know, ask Mina!" Tosha then walked over and stabbed Mina on the leg and dragged it downwards. She walked back over to me and started stabbing me again. I ran to the closet as she chased me into it still stabbing me. She left; I then came out the closet. She had her gun in her hand, pointing it at me while I was on my knees. She walked out, saying, "Once I get my gun fixed, I'll be back." I went to look for her toothbrush and it was in her drawer in her bedroom. I told her and she just got angry.

I went to Mina to ask if she were okay, and she just got angry at the fact that I got her stabbed and walked away. That morning, Tosha sat on the toilet crying, "I almost killed my baby." That's how I found out she pulled the trigger. The whole time since I began getting beaten, no one, not even my siblings, asked if I were alright. I had to cry and cope alone. I didn't get a therapist, nor did I tell anyone what was going on. In my head, we needed her to survive, and I would die if I left her care.

Tosha started driving trucks during this time and was always gone. I remember breaking a lid that went to an oil lamp. Scared of what Tosha might do to me, I used a piece of broken glass to cut my wrist. During this time, I wasn't scared to die. I felt I had stared death in the face ever since I was born. I attempted suicide twice by taking a bunch of my brother's ADHD medicine. The first time, I passed out, and the second time, I paralyzed myself from the waist down. I was outside walking to the store when my legs gave out. Mina found me and laughed, then a cop I had a crush on at the time helped me get back home. No one asked if I were alright, and they started calling me Bambi.

*I do not support suicide, I believe that if you can just hold on a little longer there is light at the end of the tunnel. I used to tell myself that, if you're in the darkness, it means you are the light.*

The following year, my junior year, I decided to join the band, and we were getting a new director.

# CHAPTER 5

# Mr. House

**The summer leading into my junior year,** our new band director was introduced; his name was Troy House. Little did I know that this man was going to be the catalyst in my life.

We were introduced in the library of my high school. Looking back, I knew I was in love the moment I met him. His curly brown hair and glasses weren't my ideal type. He walked in an apologized for being late, but he was dealing with a little hydroplaning on his way up here. He came and sat right across from me, and we began asking him questions related to the band. I couldn't take my eyes off him. He seemed cold and comforting at the same time. My soul knew him, but I had yet to learn him.

Months go by and we were in band camp. My sister had become the drum major. I remember dancing around with his sister Lena, who was a year younger than me. Up until this point, all my friends were my friends out of convenience because they wanted to be friends with Mina. She was my best friend and I looked forward to seeing her and her brother every day. We would listen to K-pop together and she would teach me new dances. Troy and I would share animes with each other and talk about things that interested us. For periods of time, we would make prolonged eye contact. I believe this made me fall in love with him. He asked me why it was so hard for me to keep eye contact. I didn't have an answer for him at that time.

I remember he was leading a lap around the school, and I was following him. I wanted to be near him no matter what. I had asthma but that didn't matter, I stayed right behind him as the rest of the band fell behind. When he turned around and realized he had left the band, we both stopped and waited for them to catch up. After the lap, we'd go to eat and sit inside as we cooled down. While we were inside, I would play around with him, I remember reaching for him and him saying, "You're in my personal space." That's when I realized that we were two separate people. I couldn't just assume he wanted me as much as I wanted him.

Once he found out I couldn't read music, he began teaching me. I was his first student.

*At the time I didn't see this as romantic, but now I do.*

We sat at the piano as he played the notes; I had to guess if they were different. I got them right until he realized I was looking at the keyboard as he played. He told me to close my eyes as he played and then guess. I don't know if I got them right after that, but I felt we had gotten closer.

He and Mina would always talk privately and that would make me jealous. I hated when he spent time with another female if it weren't his mom or sister. There was another girl who I knew liked him; her name was Deja. She swore to me that she didn't like him even though I knew she was lying. They would spend time together all the time and he would look at her like he was attracted to her. I could feel I was losing him to her, but I didn't know what to do. I was afraid to share my emotions about the matter with him.

Sometimes we'd play Uno or chess with each other. I loved the way he focused on the board. I loved any emotion he displayed. Anger, sadness, frustration, happiness, and even when he had an ego. It didn't matter, I loved his soul, and no one could change my mind.

I was a virgin, but I knew what I liked. I shared my interest in BDSM with him and he didn't seem to be shocked by it. We both took the test, and he turned out to be a master. He showed me his results happily and I hid mine. I was a slave. He said, "When two become one," while making sexual motions. We continued flirting with each other. He even called me babe in front of the whole class. He didn't care that he would lose his job.

Soccer season rolled around, and he asked me where I was going. I told him to practice, and he stated he wanted me to stay at band practice. I said, "It's my passion, Troy." He replied, "We'll go be with your passion then, Mimi." I went down to the soccer field; after band practice ended, he came down.

We had a new coach, Coach Nick. Coach Nick had made Troy assistant coach without my knowledge, and he came to every practice and drove us to games. One night after a game, I remember playing soccer with him and his sister until they turned the lights out. It was another romantic night. I fell so hard for this man it was ridiculous.

At the end of band season, we had a party. We got all dressed up and received awards. I remember his smile; it was so bright as he called my name. We danced and I ended up dragging him to the floor and him crowd surfing. After, he did one of his frat dances with one of his brothers. Deja ran by, stating how hot he was. It broke my heart, so I kept my distance.

My birthday had rolled around, and we invited the band out skating. We listened to music and enjoyed our night. Troy did a Naruto ninja run and I watched him nerd out. I remember singing Dangerous woman by Arianna Grande.

I had to take a test for my advanced English class. He came walking down the hill. I found out that a proctor was missing and because he was at the school, they asked him to proctor. While taking the exam, he'd come and stand in front of me and mess with me. I would giggle and playfully buck at him.

The next year Deja graduated, and I became a senior. We went to her graduation party and Troy was coming. She asked him to wear all white, but he wore red, blue, and black. He sat near me, and we talked as she sung Beyonce to him. He ignored her and just stared at me. I told him I had to go, and he asked me not to leave. I didn't want to, but Tosha wanted us home.

Rumor circulated that they were engaged and planning a wedding. Deja texted me asking how to meditate and I told her. Not understanding why she would ask that. I now know it was to win Troy over. She then asked me about twin flames and what they were. I told her and I said, "Me and Troy are twin flames." She ignored it and continued seeing him. I got distant from him and started to guard my heart. I knew his plans with her even though he told me we would get married and go to Japan together. We even started learning Japanese together.

I told him I lust more that I love, and I hurt him. We started getting distant and I started to work and worry more about what would happen after high school was over for me. I let him go even though I still loved him. He would visit my job and purposely order something he knew I had to make.

On his birthday, I wrote him a love poem in Japanese and made his favorite, brownies. I think I gave him food poisoning, but it was never mentioned to me. The few days he was off work were the hardest cause I just wanted to see him. I hated when he had substitutes.

One night, I was texting Troy and I asked him how he felt about me, and he said, "How do you think I feel?" I was hesitant to say anything, but I said, "I'm the best thing that ever happened to you." I then stated, "it's obvious that I care about you." However, I don't think it was obvious to him. Even my buddy at the time Alex said, "Everyone knows how you feel about Troy." The next day at school it had snowed, and my bus was running late. I was glad because I got to stay with Troy a little longer. We were standing outside the band room waiting for them to call out that my bus had arrived. I looked up at Troy and he mouthed, "I love you." Shocked that the man I loved, loved me back I stared at him. He then grabbed my bags and said, "I'll be a sub for you."

We walked to the cafeteria and sat down. He asked me if I listen to dubstep, I pretended not to hear because I didn't know what it was. They announced my bus's arrival and I left.

That Sunday, I went out to eat with my pastor to Cracker Barrell. I looked at Mina and asked, "Why does it feel like Troy has been here?" she told me that he just went on a date with Deja there. It broke my heart, but I sucked it up while we were out to eat with the pastor.

Later that day, I texted Troy using a scenario to get my point across. I stated that I loved him, and that Deja was just using him for attention. He asked why I would love him if I didn't even know him. A valid question but I'm not one who ignores my heart. I began crying and Tosha called Troy and cussed him out. That was when I feel we both gave up on trying.

Deja went to college and Troy would often visit her. One day, they had sex and he had broken up with her. She called me crying, saying, "Troy and I did something and after, he broke up with me." I knew by the way she was crying what had taken place and for the first but not the last time I audibly heard my heart tare in half. I felt a pain close to being stabbed, shoot through my body. I told Deja she could have him and that I wouldn't stop her anymore.

# CHAPTER 6

# Adulthood

**Now my sister lived with her boyfriend** and had a baby on the way. It was just me and Tosha. No one was there to witness or stop the abuse. One day, she asked me to pick between living with her or keeping my job. I heard God's voice say, "I will kill her." I began crying because I knew telling her I would leave meant that I would have to figure out how to survive on my own. I told her that God said he would kill me if I stayed. That's the only way I knew she would let me go. I packed my things and headed into work. I called my sister's boyfriend's mother Reda and asked her if I could stay. She accepted and I offered to pay rent. I was okay with that because Tosha was taking more money than Reda had asked for.

Mina's boyfriend Marcus was in jail, and I would send money to him so that they could talk. After, my niece Mimi #2 was born.

*We're going to call her #2.*

I would lay on the floor and rock her to sleep. It was like she became my daughter. I would spend time with her when I wasn't at work, and she grew up fast.

I was sleeping on the floor of Reda's apartment, working and trying to get into college. I got accepted into Livingstone college with a full ride. I played in the band and majored in culinary. College wasn't really my cup of tea. In fact, I really hated school. I didn't know how much I hated school until I was no longer being abused. I ended up getting alcohol poisoning and taken to the hospital. I woke up in the bed and asked the nurse how I got there. He told me I had alcohol poisoning and that an ambulance had brought me. I screamed internally, because I knew from Mina passing out how expensive it was. They did a few checkups, then gave me a free ride back to campus. I slept in my friend's room, and he bought me something to eat so that I could feel better.

Livingstone was Troy's old college, and he would come and visit at band practices. The first time he came, he introduced Deja, and mention that she was his wife. He knew I went to Livingstone because he was there when I first got on campus, and he jokingly said, how I was moving into the thot's dorm hall.

Second semester rolled in, and I was taken off campus to a hotel to take my culinary classes. This was in 2019 before covid really hit. At the time, I was in an on-again, off-again relationship with this girl named Reilly. I ended up taking her virginity, even though I had plans to lose mine in marriage. She would sometimes hit me when I didn't want to have sex with her. I would ask her to never hit me again stating that I had been abused growing up and she told me she wouldn't.

In December, for the Christmas break, I went to her dad's place and stayed with them. She told me he was a little racist, but at the time he was one of the most open-minded people I had ever talked to. I would sit in the living room and talk about politics and music. He grew weed in his house and he would smoke it to calm himself down. At this point, I was smoking and drinking as well. I never told Reilly that I smoked, until I seen his plants. We would go on dates and spend so much time together. She went to UNCC, and I was there more than I was at my own college. She showed me the soccer field and I was kind of jealous because Livingstone didn't have a soccer team. We ate at her cafeteria and stayed in her dorm room trying to figure out how to get rich quick.

Covid came and they forced all the culinary majors off campus. I prayed to God to help me because I knew I would have nowhere to go. I ended up moving back in with Reda. I used my college refund check to buy a car. Mina and Marcus mostly used the car even though it was mine.

Mina's ex, Jinx, who was also her ex-best friend asked me if I wanted to move in with her and her new girlfriend, Audrey. I agreed because I was tired of being homeless and ready to live by my own rules. Plus, Marcus always had a problem with me. I asked Reilly if she wanted to move with us and she did.

By this time, I had a new job working for a distribution center making more money than I knew what to do with. I used the surplus of money to buy weed. The apartment we chose to move into cost us all $1,373 a month.

Before the first month, Reilly had a problem with her and I paying most of the bill. Jinx and Audrey both got into an argument with Reilly's sister, T. T told them that they shouldn't be making us pay a thousand while they only paid $373. The issue was settled, and we split the bill evenly. While living with them, all I did was work and smoke. Sometimes I would smoke at work, on my breaks. I broke up with Reilly officially and she moved out. I switched rooms with Jinx and Audrey, and it would continue like that for the remainder of the lease.

# CHAPTER 7

# The Awakening

**After I got my new job at the distribution center,** I met this girl named A.J. She became my best friend, and I would always spend time with her. I found out she had the same birthday as Troy. After we got off work at 0430, we would go to waffle house. I would sit in her car during breaks, and she would tell me stories about her ex-boyfriend. I would listen to her rant about how much she loved him and about the abuse he put her through. A.J had no problem with getting boyfriends.

After some time passed, I got back in contact with Troy's mother, Chris, and Lina. They mentioned how he had caught covid and that night I prayed for him again. Soon after that, I texted Deja and I asked her how she was, and she mentioned that she was filling out some paperwork so that she and Troy could get married. I asked her if I could get closure and I stated that he asked for my soul while we were still in high school, and we shook on it. She said it was rude of me to ask for closure from her husband and that I should not contact them again. I texted him on messenger that I still loved him, and I wrote him a love poem on his YouTube channel. In the poem, I told him that my love would last an eternity.

After that, I looked up ways to bring your twin flame in faster. I began seeing his name everywhere. I even had tarot readings done to see if he were really my twin flame. I stumbled on a video that said something that really took me by surprise. It said, that in order to get your twin flame you had to heal your traumas and become one within yourself. I knew then what I had to do.

I began journaling and wrote down all my deepest traumas. Sort of like how I wrote them down in this book. However, in my journal, my D.I.D showed. I let each personality talk and I worked through all my traumas. The video led in a meditation session and open the door to my psyche. I ran out the room to Jinx and cried, "My mother stabbed me." She laughed and said jokingly, "Yeah, but you been known that." She then realized I was really in pain and gave me a hug. After that day, I kept journaling and working through my trauma, it felt good.

One day, I went on break and saw a message from Troy stating that I should not reach out to him again and that he did not love me. After that, I went back into work and was introduced to a man by this lady named Bunny. The guy's name was Tony. That night after work, I went home and took a shower. I then got dressed and went over to Tony's place. He rolled a blunt and we smoked in my car. I lost my virginity that night. I then kicked him out my car and drove away. The next day, he saw that I wore a revealing shirt and he said, "Oh, so today, you want to have your breast out?" He had told me right before we had sex that he didn't want me, so I chuckled and said, "Yeah." I got on my forklift and drove away.

After that, I had sex with eight different men. I stopped because none of them wanted me, and I was still in love with Troy. I went back to my old band to help because Jinx wanted to help the dancers get better. I tried helping the band, but became disappointed by the music and the effort the students put in. I then had a student text Troy to see if we could get his music.

One day while Audrey and I entered a Japanese restaurant, a man overheard our conversation about passions. He said, "Passions? That's a good topic for discussion," and he said something about Audrey's passion to workout. I wanted to hear what he was going to say about mine, so I told him, "My passion is music." He looked at me and said, "Well if you ever meet the devil at the crossroads, don't sell your soul." Audrey and I went to be seated.

I continued journaling, meditating, and praying. Around this time, A.J. had introduced me to coke. At first, I was afraid, but then as time went on, I did it with no problem. She then bought acid and I tried it right before work. When I went into work, I notice that my anger was stronger than normal and while I was walking, I was shocking one of my co-workers. I mentioned how I was on acid, and I was angry, so that's why he was getting shocked. I calmed down and I got the equipment I was looking for. I got on my forklift and continued doing my job. It seemed like everyone was affected by me being on acid. I could sense people around me and I could basically drive my forklift without having to look.

People began watching and analyzing me. That's when the voices started. I could hear people talking about me but when I brought it up, they pretended like they didn't know what I was talking about. I soon realized that it was their souls talking and not them. I knew things that people would later figure out, and I would guess things and people would freak out when it turned out to be true.

One day, I went to the beach with A.J and our new friend Chuck. I could tell that he was sexually attracted to me, but I wouldn't let my guard down. I knew he was waiting for me to fall asleep so that he could have his way with me, and I knew A.J was trying to let him. On this trip, we met up with one of our friends, Susan, and her family. We did coke in the bathroom. This time it looked a little wet, but I didn't question it. The night that Chuck would try to have his way I stayed up watching murder mysteries on tv. He got annoyed claiming that when I talked, I would wake him up. Because my gifts were heightened, I knew that he was up the entire time. We ended up going home early and I brought it up to them. They lied stating that wasn't their intentions and I cut ties with them.

I would get downloads of information, and my gift to see in the spirit realm was heightened. My roommates were gone to New York, and I was home alone. I went into my roommate's room and texted Troy that I loved him one more time. He texted back after realizing it was me and stated that he didn't love me again, and because I reached back out to him, he would contact the authorities and have them handle the situation.

That night, I turned on the red lights in my roommate's room and sent my soul to hell. I watched as shadows passed and then a hand came and covered my face. I heard a voice say, "Your demon is here." I knew that now I was talking with the devil. I said, "About time what took so long –." I closed my eyes and opened them again and said, "And next time come humbly." A light shined in his eye, and I closed mine. I was now in hell. I looked at him and for some reason I felt a sense of love. I said, "I want you to bring me the man I love, Troy House." He asked, "What would I get in return, your soul?" I speedily said, "No, my heart." He looked at me, and I could tell I had met this man before, because our connection was natural, like we were in love before. He accepted my offer and asked if I were Persephone. I left hell.

While listening to the radio, I would tap into the spirit realm and people would begin talking to or about me. It was like reality was synced to my thoughts. I would listen to music and people would sing about how they were happy to be alive when I was alive.

I began trying to translate the bible. I remember my reality morphing and I knew I was breaking through the matrix. During this time, I would take walks around my apartment. I would hear people say from their apartments, "Jesus is real!" Every time, I was led to the city park in Salisbury. I would end up at Tosha's house after that. One day at the park, I entered hell again and the devil returned my heart, stating that he could not bring Troy to me. I got up and began weeping, and rain started pouring down. I lost the key to my car and Tosha took me back to my apartment. I was led back to the park, and there was when my veil lifted. I was into the spirit realm completely and I found out not all people were humans and there was more to life than what meets the eye. I kept getting downloads at this time. All I remember was wanting Troy the entire time.

One day, while I was at the park, I ended up walking to Tosha's house. I didn't have on anything, but a hoodie and I would ask a man for a ride the rest of the way because my feet were getting stabbed by things on the ground. I got there and Tosha punched me in the face. She called Mina to come get me and when she came, I tried to explain what I was going through. I told her I was being tested by God and that I was just following orders. Tosha and Mina discussed taking me somewhere and I just told Tosha to watch. I tried to meditate to calm down. When I looked up, Tosha's current husband, Ron, Marcus, and Mina were all looking at me. Like they were drained of life. Tosha's screamed and started crying. That day she took me to the hospital.

I entered the hospital, and they took a urine test on me. That's when I found out I had fentanyl in my system. They allowed me to speak with a doctor on a computer screen and Tosha kept trying to change my truth. By this time, I learned not to let her do that, So I spoke over her, repeating what I had said to the doctor. They removed Tosha as she kept saying that I was lying. After the call with the doctor, I laid down and fell asleep. When I woke back up, an old lady was sitting in a chair in front of my bed. She said, "God?" and I responded, "Yes?" she said, "I knew it was you." She then asked if I would follow a doctor to another section of the hospital. As I walked with the other doctor, I passed a pillar and I no longer saw her.

When I entered a new area of the hospital, they gave me a room with personal care items. I sat in the room. I looked at the swans they had made from the towels, but at that time, I interpreted them as snakes. I looked at my hand which was wrapped in my hoodie, and I stated that it was a possession. The nurses then rushed in and asked for all my clothes. They gave me clothes to change into and asked me to take a shower. I did as I was told.

I attended meetings while I was there, and I remember being in an AA meeting and they were all stating why they were there. I couldn't look at them while they were talking because they would stutter and forget what they were saying. I had to allow my eyes to drift around the room and afterwards a lady stated how she probably wasn't being honest in the parts stated when I was looking at her. The guy sitting across from me stared at me in amazement. After the meeting, we ate and had free time. I would color. There was this girl there that I couldn't get a grip on and another woman there that I thought I met at the crossroads. I would continue getting downloads. I knew everyone there was affected by my veil opening.

I remember waking up in the middle of the night and seeing the door morph from normal into a heaven gate. I heard a nurse say, "She's smart." I also remember hearing two claps and my body jumped out of bed. I walked into the hallway and all the nurses were frozen in place. I thought this meant I could escape but the doors were locked, and the people began moving again. A nurse showed up and told me I couldn't leave and shouldn't be in that area. I headed back to my room.

I played chess with one of the ladies that I was in there with, and a guy told her moves to make. I mentioned how I hate playing chess against someone who had a coach. I beat her and we then went into the other room. I heard the guy say, "Well, if you're going to use me, you've got to share." I stuck my hand into the crayons bucket and read a color it said, 'yellow snake.' I knew it was referencing the guy. After a while, I met up with this psychologist and she took me to a room full of people and I could see their souls. I kept asking, "Is this a church?" The room felt holy to me. After we left, she looked at me and said, "How long have you had these powers?" I stated that I started seeing things recently and she repeated her question saying, "How long have you had these powers?" I said, "Since birth, my veil just wasn't open." She walked me back to the room.

I remember calling Troy and asking him to come get me. I even made him the person that was supposed to check me out of the hospital. Tosha told the hospital before I was admitted that I thought this whole thing was a set up to marry Troy. I called him again a couple days later, but his voice sounded deep and different.

I remember calling some of the nurses angels while I was there. I took my medicine that was for schizophrenia, and I could feel the energy leaving my brain. I knew that some medicines were meant to suppress spiritual gifts. It was fine with me; I just wanted to leave. Tosha came, and for the first time we talked about the time she stabbed me. She told me she thought she stabbed the wall, and she asked if I would forgive her. That day I honestly forgave her. Eventually, I came up with a plan that I would do after I got out and showed a nurse. The next day, I was released. They sent me home with two prescriptions that I would take. My roommates were home after I got out and Jinx was happy to see me. She was mad that I never told her about the drugs I was taking. She and Mina got into an argument, and I defended Mina, even though I told Mina it wasn't Jinx's fault.

A couple days passed, and I went to get my medicine from Walmart. The voices were still loud, and I could hear people say, "She is God." I went and got my medicine and then left. By this time, I had quit my job at the distribution center and couldn't pay the rent. Jinx and Audrey covered my portion, and after I got a job, I paid them back. At first, I wanted to move out, because Jinx was trying to steal my energy. I used to draw a symbol in my notebooks, and one day, Jinx caught a glimpse of it. I felt all the power in my body drain out of me. I could barely lift my hand to grab the blunt. When Jinx saw this, all she said was, "We're going to make money tonight." She had just transitioned into being a stripper. That hurt, and from then on, I knew that I couldn't trust her.

Every time I smoked, my veil would open and I knew it. Audrey seemed to have no idea what was going on. However, our drug dealer at the time was affected by it and so was Jinx. He saw something that occurred between me and Audrey that she didn't even notice. He laughed, saying, "Ahhhh, the gray area." After this, he tried not to make eye contact with me.

I later got a job at McDonald's, and there my veil would have free reign. This time, it wasn't voices; it was the actual people talking about me. A girl ran up to me and said, "Thank you for picking McDonald's." I could tell people were trying to get a grip on me but couldn't. People came and looked at me, and families would just smile, with light in their eyes. Someone asked if I were a witch. I'm not, but I jokingly said, "Don't tell the priest." He freaked out and walked away. They tried to teach people how to steal my energy, but that would only upset me. It's my energy, why do you think you have the right to it? It made me furious. I ended up walking out after one of the managers arrogantly tried to steal my energy. As I was walking out, one of the ladies asked me what was wrong and I said, "Y'all keep playing with me, acting like I don't know that y'all are stealing my energy." She tried to trick me and told me that she didn't know what I was talking about and the man she was talking to was hoping that I would get fooled. I said back to her, "No! I'm not dumb I know when you have my energy because your eyes are darker." That's when her eyes went back to the original color, which was a light brown. The man freaked out and went outside.

While I was walking home, I saw the dark figure again. He was following me. I had a dream that he was reaching out for me; I felt his power surge through my body. I screamed for my mom. That was the first time I had sleep paralysis inside of a dream.

I wanted to go to the marine reserves so that I could have enough money to fulfill my purpose. I also loved working out. Deep inside, I knew I was joining the marines so that I could kill people legally. They never got back to me after I ran the mile and a half 30 seconds short. I then tried the army, and because I had weed in my system, I had to wait. It ended up taking four months to clear my system, and by that time, I got a speeding ticket and had to wait longer to be sent to basic training.

During this time, I went back to Tosha's house and cleaned up Mina's room. To be honest, it still had junk in there from when I shared a room with her, but I also had to clean her trash. I could tell that the two worlds were merged, in fact they always were. I started being aware of the strange things that happened. It was easy for me to understand why certain things happened and I was no longer ignorant to my reality. I knew my purpose and I was just ready to do it.

While waiting to start my new job, I received a restraining order from the sheriff. It was from Troy. Deja and Lena already got theirs and I had to go to court for his. I found out they pressed charges on me, while I was in the hospital, but I couldn't go to court. I also found out that Lina lied stating that I was stalking her at our old school during their band practices which was a lie. I went to court, and they had to reschedule because he couldn't make it. They said he was overseas, and for the second time, I felt my heart rip. I heard a voice say, "He wanted them to go together." I left the courthouse, and it was raining hard. I went back home and cried. Audrey and Jinx came in and tried to comfort me.

I went to court again and I finally got to see him again. The love that I had for that man had not died. When I saw him, a smile stretched across my face. He basically begged the judge for the order to go through, but she stated that there was no valid reason and I had to be threatening him. He stated that there was never anything between us and he wanted to stay with his wife.

Later that day, Audrey showed me pictures of Deja and Troy's wedding on Instagram. By that time, I had promised the judge I wouldn't contact him. All I could do was cry, like how could you be happy without me. I was in shock, that I existed without him. It left this longing in my heart for him that came with the after taste of bitterness.

I kept taking my medicine and experienced almost the same thing, no matter where I went. I eventually calmed down and my veil adjusted. I went to work at a UPS warehouse. It was an easy job, but I hated waking up at 0200 just to go to work. All my pay-checks went to Audrey and Jinx until I paid off the debt that I gathered while being out of work.

Time passed and the end of our lease came. I helped them move out and then I moved myself out. Our drug dealer helped me move out and I was basically homeless again living with my aunt in her one bedroom. I would drive her to two places and would run errands for Alicia. My gifts were back to normal, but I could still here the voices. Living with my aunt was killing me and I couldn't wait to have my own place. I was ready to start living my dreams and every day that I couldn't seemed like a chore to me. I could tell that my family had a problem with drug abuse, and it really hindered them. After a while, I stop smoking and I stopped doing the other drugs all together. I bounced back and forth from Zina's to Mina's place

We would spend time together and go out. Eventually, Sasha got me a place to stay at these apartments she rented. I would drive back and forth from Kannapolis to Salisbury to see them. After a while, I got into a wreck and lost my car. Sasha or Mina would come pick me up and bring me back. By this time, I had slept with 13 men and was seeing one of them, John.

I had dreams of my sisters forcing me to eat meat, even when they knew I was vegetarian. Remember, I understood more than a typical person about the spirit realm. So, I cut them all off. Sasha came and got her washer and dryer, and they all said that I had used them. I finally transitioned over to being vegan. One night, I went to John's place while he was cross faded, and we chilled, watching the P. J's. We talked and he mentioned how he only lived to kill and cause chaos. I watched as his face morphed into a centaur. He then climbed on top of me and that's how I knew he wanted to have sex. We started having sex and I felt the life drain from my body. I cut him off, and I had only God. I didn't want to have contact with anyone who wasn't in the plans God had for me. I became celibate and tried not to think about sex. It became easier to fast and pray and the spiritual warfare didn't affect me as much. I knew when certain people treated me a certain way what they wanted, and I knew that if they had a problem with me, they were the problem.

By this time, I became manager at my first job, Bojangles, and I had gotten transferred to a new location in Kannapolis. It happened to be in walking distance from my apartment.

# CHAPTER 8

# Self-love / Fully Healed

**Living alone, I had cut all my family off.** I was still seeing Troy's name and I thought, I'll just ignore it. For the first time, I was happy to be alive and I loved myself more than ever. When I found myself being goofy, I would say, "Omg I love you," and realize I was talking to myself. I loved all my personality traits even my anger issues. I loved the way I was free spirited, the way I loved everyone unconditionally. I analyzed myself and every time I found out something new about myself, I loved it. I began writing and singing again. Some people loved my voice and others hated it. I didn't care, it wasn't my battle to fight. I learned that I no longer had to adjust myself so that others felt comfortable. If they didn't like me, it was their problem. I learned that if I filtered myself that I wasn't loving myself. The only person I cared about loving, and accepting me, was God.

People seemed to hate the fact that I was at peace. I still had miles to go before I was fully awake, but at this point the mountains felt like hills and the obstacles fell at my feet. No one could stop me from becoming one within myself not even my love for Troy. I told God, "I don't care what I must get rid of, even if it's my love for Troy. I will fulfill my purpose." After that, it seemed like everything came into alignment for me and I started working on my talents. I learned that I always knew what I had to do, I just didn't know why. I was pleased with that revelation, and I kept on fighting demons and those unseen enemies; however, the unseen enemies were now seen, and they stood no chance. I knew that every demon and malnourished spirit stood no chance against me.

## Currently

I don't own a tv, but I know what time we are in. I do not get angry at those who aren't aware of the sprit realm. Nor do I get angry at the voices. I pity them, because I know what is coming and if you're not actively fighting for God, I pray that you begin. I'm only 21, but I know that many people live a mundane life not knowing that the battle we fight is a spiritual one. You might think it's just normal, but I have seen pass the matrix into reality.

You can either choose to trust my words or toss this book aside but I'm telling you, just because you ignore it doesn't mean it's not there. I remember watching a movie, and in it a girl asked her father. "How do you know if you're a good person?" He responded, "Well, it depends on what wolf you feed, the good, or the bad one." I know now that the bad wolf is your flesh and earthly desires, and the good is your spirit. Don't let the comfort of the world keep you from living the happiest and most abundant life you could ever live.